DATE DUE

THE WEATHER
OF SIX MORNINGS

The Lamont Poetry Selection for 1968
of The Academy of American Poets

This distinguished award, sponsored
"for the discovery and encouragement
of new poetic genius," is made every year
to an American poet who has not yet had
a book of poetry published. The judges
for 1968 were Hayden Carruth, Donald Hall,
Donald Justice, William E. Stafford
and James Wright.

THE WEATHER OF SIX MORNINGS

POEMS

by Jane Cooper

THE MACMILLAN COMPANY

COLLIER-MACMILLAN LTD., LONDON

FIRST PRINTING

The Macmillan Company
Collier-Macmillan Canada Ltd, Toronto, Ontario

Printed in the United States of America

ACKNOWLEDGMENTS

Some of these poems first appeared in the following magazines and antho-
logies, to whose editors grateful acknowledgment is made: *The Antioch
Review, New World Writing 11, Poetry London—New York, Sarah Lawrence Alumnae Magazine, Sarah Lawrence Journal, The Transatlantic Review, Voices, Voyages; American Poems* (Southern Illinois University
Press, ed. J. Kessler), *Modern Occasions* (Farrar, Straus and Giroux, ed. P.
Rahv), *New Poets of England and America, Second Selection* (Meridian
Books, ed. D. Hall and R. Pack). "The Builder of Houses" first appeared
in *Poetry* (Chicago). The poems "Morning on the St. John's" (in a
slightly different version), "The Weather of Six Mornings," "No More
Elegies," and "Feathers" (under the title "March") appeared originally
in *The New Yorker*.

I wish to thank the John Simon Guggenheim Memorial Foundation, the
Corporation of Yaddo, the MacDowell Colony, and Mrs. E. S. Merriman
for giving the freedom and thoughtful aid that made many of these poems
possible.

CONTENTS

III *Blue Spaces*

Her is non hoom, her nis but wildernesse:
Forth, pilgrim, forth! Forth, beste, out of thy stal!
Know thy contree, look up, thank God of al. . . .

I

March

March

1 | FEATHERS

I've died, but you are still living.
The pines are still living, and the eastern sky.
Today a great bustle rocks the treetops
of snow and sunshine, dry branches, green brooms.

The pines are cleaning their attics.
Mercilessly, they snap off weak twigs.
If I look down from my window
I can see one of the walks we used to take together.

The snow is covered with brown feathers.
In the fields it's as if an army had just limped by,
leaving its slight corpses, abandoned weapons—
a wreckage that will melt into spring.

Nearby is a little grove; on brown needles
we lay side by side telling each other stories.
As long as I do not go there
nothing can stop the huzzah of the male wind!

The last full moon of February
stalks the fields; barbed wire casts a shadow.
Rising slowly, a beam moved toward the west
stealthily changing position

until now, in the small hours, across the snow
it advances on my pillow
to wake me, not rudely like the sun
but with the cocked gun of silence.

I am alone in a vast room
where a vain woman once slept.
The moon, in pale buckskins, crouches
on guard beside her bed.

Slowly the light wanes, the snow will melt
and all the fences thrum in the spring breeze
but not until that sleeper, trapped
in my body, turns and turns.

3 | EL SUEÑO DE LA RAZÓN

(for a young poet in a mental hospital)

Cousin, it's of you I always dream
as I walk these dislocated lawns
or compose a stanza under the Corot trees.

The music of my walking reconciles
somewhat the clipped but common ground
with the lost treetops' thunderous heads.

How they are always muttering in the still
afternoon; how they create
their own darkness under hottest sun.

They compose clouds or a sea
so far above us we can scarcely tell
why such a premonition brushes our cheeks.

Yet as I walk I scan
the woods for a girl's white figure
slipping away among the pines' thin shafts.

Hiding, she is hiding, and in your dreams
the poem's cleared spaces
barely hold out against the stately riot

of marching trees, a suddenly Turner sky.
Poor furious girl, our voices sound
alike (your nurse told me), discreet and gentle.

4 | RETURN

I was prepared for places
as someone packs bags against hell,
meditating on each jolt of memory
before I stumbled over it.

Secretly I rehearsed the stages
of our coming to know one another,
furnished each scene with trees,
even a phoebe calling.

So I preserved a wintry face
as I returned little by little
to the rooms where we slept, the closet
where you hung your worn raincoat.

But tonight it's all sham—
From her hidden alcove a woman
hums that aria of Purcell's
tentatively, sweetly:

Dido is pleading, Aeneas
blurs into her past, his future.
Again your eyes star
with salt as I choose my elegy.

5 | NO MORE ELEGIES

Today the snow crunches underfoot
and squeaks dryly like compressed sugar.
Up the road run tire ribbons,
along the paths the quick prints of rabbits.

Everyone rushed into town
right after coffee, though the icy ruts
are gray as iron, and icicles
two feet long scarcely drip.

The sun is so bright on the snow
I'm out tramping in dark beach glasses.
A clump of leafless birches
steams against a dark blue sky.

Over there the yellow frame
of some new construction glints,
while the tips of those bushes are bloody
as if tomorrow, tomorrow would be Easter!

And a phoebe is calling, calling,
all the small birds come fluting from the pines:
"No more elegies, no more elegies!" Poor
fools, they don't know it's not spring!

As a boy he was so silent
she raged like a gnat. Summer nights—

Summer nights he stood at his desk
wrapped in a wordless soprano.

Once he constructed a clipper ship
to scale from the *Century Dictionary.*

All May they ran barefoot
through the stinging southern streets.

The air was like mercury,
a heavy silver ball.

And the river stank of salt
and rotten magnolia candles

down the end of the block—Slot machines!
From their grandmother's veranda

she could hear the ring of life
start out through a swing door—

No one could tell such stories;
but he never cried, not once.

7 | MIDDLE AGE

At last it's still—a gray thaw.
Who ever saw a more sullen day?
On the porch, among patches of standing water,
a bluejay pecks at an uncovered seed.

It's not even raining. In the vanished night
a brief snow fell, dampening the paths.
The paths are brown with ashes—
or is it the first earth showing through?

The pines are at rest. I'm waiting—
oh, for some insight, some musical phrase,
for the voices of my friends,
for faint traffic noises from the far-off city,

for choruses, for a symphony orchestra,
for the screech of a subway train rounding a bend,
a baby's ah-ah-ah
or the rich, hesitant speech of students—

How amazing to be born! A few drops
of rain slip their stones into puddles,
and circles of light ride out
smashing the icy islands—

I can't hear their splash. I'm alert
only to dreams as the rain falls harder.
Each word, each memory cracks open.
Only the miracle is real.

9

An air of departures. Silences.
Again the pines are sheathed in a wet snow.
The chimney breathes its slow, transparent smoke.

Everything has been offered, nothing given.
Everything, not the first thing has been said.
After me who will sit here, patiently writing?

Words over a page: a slow smoke
scrolling across the sky what is unconsumed
by the deep, thunderous fires of the house—

An air of departures. Now the tall city
stoops to receive us, where we blur like snow
leaving behind a breath of loves and angers.

II

Imaginary
Houses

Morning on the St. John's

*(The Chinese character for landscape is mountains-and-water.
A Japanese image of heaven is Fuji reflected in a pool.)*

This is a country where there are no mountains:
At dawn the water birds like lines of rain
Rise from the penciled grasses by the river
And slantwise creak across the growing light.
The sky lifts upward and the breath of flowers
Wakes with the shadows of the waking birds.

The shadows of the birds, the dancing birds!
With so much freedom who could ask for mountains?
The heron stands here ankle-deep in flowers,
Wet hyacinths that burn more blue with rain,
And waves of smaller wings hurl wide the light
All up and down the horizontal river.

And now the sun shakes blue locks in the river
And rises dripping-headed while the birds
Go wild in curves of praise at sudden light.
The fire that would flash instantly off mountains
Bathes this round world in dew as dark as rain
And then strikes green and gold among the flowers.

The dropping heads, the smooth and shaken flowers!
(Among the grasses, blue eyes by the river,
And in the garden, fires after rain.)

Under umbrella leaves the mockingbirds
Still nestle and trill quietly of mountains,
Then whistle Light!—cadenza—Light! and Light!

While higher and higher sweeps the opening light
In bluish petals as of opening flowers,
More pure than snow at dawn among the mountains.
Paler than any flush along the river,
Beyond the reach of eyefall flight of birds,
It floods a sky swept innocent by rain.

The assault of sun, the long assault of rain—
Look how our darkness is made true by light!
Look how our silence is confirmed by birds!
The mind that pastured ankle-deep in flowers
Last night, must wake to sunrise on the river,
Graze wide and then grow vertical as mountains;

For even a glimpse of mountains fogged with rain
Or mirrored in a river brings delight
And shakes a man as dawn shakes birds and flowers.

Obligations

Here where we are, wrapped in the afternoon
As in a chrysalis of silken light,
Our bodies kindly holding one another
Against the press of vision from outside,
Here where we clasp in a stubble field
Is all the safety either of us hopes for,
Stubbornly constructing walls of night
Out of the ordered energies of the sun.

With the same gratitude I feel the hot
Dazzle on my eyelids and your hand
Carefully opening my shaded breasts.
The air is very high and still. The buzz
And tickle of an insect glow and fuse
Into the flicker of a pulse. We rest
Closed in the golden shallows of a sound.
Once, opening my eyes, I betray your trust.

Startled, I break apart a shining blade
Of stubble as you bend to look at me.
What can your eyes lay claim to? What extreme
Unction after love is forced upon us?
The sun is setting now after its fullness
While on the horizon like a fiery dream
Wakes the long war, and shared reality,
And death and all we came here to evade.

Two Who Passed By

We saw the fire against the sky
And heard the horses screaming.
The barn roof fell as we drove by
Late in the August evening.

The sparks had put the starlight out.
We watched the ridgepole snapping
Till like a Christmas tree upset
It reared, its candles flashing,

Then dove to earth—a sudden hiss,
Hysteria doused by water.
We passed the war in love like this
And necessary laughter.

The Faithful

Once you said joking slyly, "If I'm killed
I'll come to haunt your solemn bed,
I'll stand and glower at the head
And see if my place is empty still, or filled."

What was it woke me in the early darkness
Before the first bird's twittering?
—A shape dissolving and flittering
Unsteady as a flame in a drafty house.

It seemed a concentration of the dark burning
By the bedpost at my right hand,
While to my left that no-man's land
Of sheet stretched palely as a false morning. . . .

All day I have been sick and restless. This evening
Curtained, with all the lights on,
I start up—only to sit down.
Why should I grieve after ten years of grieving?

What if last night I was the one who lay dead,
While the dead burned beside me
Trembling with passionate pity
At my blameless life and shaking its flamelike head?

For My Mother in Her First Illness, from a Window Overlooking Notre Dame

Why can I never when I think about it
See your face tender under the tasseled light
Above a book held in your stubby fingers?
Or catch your tumbling gamecock angers?
Or—as a child once, feverish by night—
Wake to your sleepless profiled granite?

But I must reconstruct you, feature by feature:
Your sailor's gaze, a visionary blue,
Not stay-at-home but wistful northern eyes;
And the nose Gothic, oversized,
Delicately groined to the eyesockets' shadow,
Proud as a precipice above laughter.

Arrogant as a cathedral or the sea
You carry your blue spaces high and quick
On a young step, tapping or chivalrous.
Pilgrim of the ridiculous
And of a beauty now almost archaic,
I miss your swift inward, your needle's eye.

Light stalk, my love is all of movement,
Those ribs of quicksand feeling in your face,
Those knowledgeable energetic gargoyles.

Still haunted by my first devils,
Alone and sick, lying in a foreign house,
How can I tell which one of us is absent?

Leaving Water Hyacinths

(on an old photograph, Jacksonville, 1933)

I see you, child, standing above the river
Like a thin bush, too young for bloom or fruit
But solidly planted, both knees locked backwards
And blue-gray eyes quietly, typically watchful:
The catboats play over a chuckling sunlight
(Funny how waves slide over, sunlight under!)
And hyacinths grip down, rooted in heaven.

I know—because you become me—you say goodby
To thumping dark paddle-like hyacinth leaves
With blood-brown stems and blue and sucking heads,
To the river's massive purr, its sustained dredge
And flap at the dock stilts (stiff, a heron's legs!)
—Sounds which can stop in air your breakfast teaspoon
Or lap as lights across the bedtime ceiling.

I know—because you contain me—you seem cool-eyed
And yet you sense that once you leave this landing
Your whole life after will be sailing back:
A seeking out of losses, the catboats' débris
Which cloud a harbor but bloom upwards blue,
And where the heron climbs, his lank limbs dropping,
Music that cradles grief to an Atlantic.

To a Very Old Man, on the Death of His Wife

(for Sara, Ivan, and Catherine)

So near to death yourself
You cannot justly mourn
For one who was beautiful
Before these children were born.
You only remember her
Poised by the edge of the sea
As you stalked heron-legged,
Chairing the baby high
(Red-capped, hilarious)
Through the ecstatic surf,
And all the boardwalk flags
Clapped to her seaward laugh.

Or perhaps she would pretend
To lose you over the edge
Of that great curve of blue
Distinct as a cliffy ledge,
And cry and wave and cry
Until with a little breath
She spied the red-capped head
Of the pledge both flung at death;
Then she would swing her hat
With her graceful arm held high
As if she would top the flags
And the flags could sweep the sky.

Now it is she who is gone
And you wait on the sand.
The place itself has changed,
The boardwalks are torn down.
For places curve with time
Over the horizon's rim;
Only a seabird flies
Lower and seems to skim
All that has been or is. . . .
No one is left to share
Those windless flags you see
Alone in the dying glare.

The Builder of Houses

(for Sally Appleton)

What was the blond child building
Down by the pond at near-dark
When the trees had lost their gilding
And the giant shadows stepped
To the water's edge, then stopped?
With intent fingers, doing a boy's work
In a boy's old sweater,
She hammered against her dear world's dirty weather.

Proud of her first house
Which boasted an orange-crate ceiling,
A pillow, a stuffed mouse,
And room for complete privacy
In the obvious crotch of a tree,
She skipped and swagged; rude cousins came stealing
With boys' laughter
And dismantled all but one branchy rafter.

She hunted almost till summer
Before her second find:
A post like a sunken swimmer
Deep in the marsh where ducks
Made nesting clucks and squawks.
With cautious tappings she fashioned a duck blind—
Or so her stepfather
Claimed when his autumn guns began to gather.

All winter in secret mourning
She toiled on her third house.
Three miles from the driveway turning
Up a forgotten path,
Risking her mother's wrath,
She tramped until her footprints filled with ice.
That bright glazing
Revealed one day her high and forbidden blazing.

In the very swaying top
Of a wind-swept sugar maple
She had built a bare prop—
Five boards to hold the crouch
Of a fugitive from search.
Here on this slippery and hard-won table,
Armed with her hammer,
She was tracked down by dogs' and parents' clamor.

There was only one more trial:
When frozen brackish March
Gave way to floods in April
She rowed a sadly leaking
Scow, its oarlocks creaking,
Out to an island in the glittering reach,
And there, halfheartedly,
Began to floor the bend of a stunted tree.

Why was this last, secluded
And never-mentioned mansion
The one she never concluded?
No one—not father nor mother
Nor even the mellowing weather—
Routed her from her chosen foothold and passion;

This time house and view
Were hers, island and vision to wander through.

But less and less she balanced
Her boat on the sunrise water
Or from her window glanced
To where that outline glimmered;
Island and house were inner,
And perhaps existed only for love to scatter
Such long, carefully planned
And sovereign childhood with its unrelenting hand.

Lunar Wonder

Such lunar wonder like a child's
Shone from her face
That he would set blind mirrors up
To multiply her grace.

Everywhere she stepped toward him
Her own face would be
Swaying like a bewildered moon
Unstable on the sea.

And every time she touched him
Hoping to be drowned
He led her to an echoing room
With mirrors all around

And gently left her there alone
Terrified by the chill,
Drooping and diminishing,
Only a child still.

A Letter for Philo Buck

(who on being sent some early poems wrote, "Don't settle for summer apples.")

I wonder are these apples ripe enough?
"My dear," you said, "no one would choose the yellow
Fruit that hangs down in August, succulent, mellow,
Ready to drop of its own weight mushily off
The branch, or vanish at a swallow.

"Wait till your own work shines like a McIntosh,
A Winesap or some stubborn little apple,
Red as a berry—not like summer squash—
Which to dislodge takes ladders or the wash
Of winter storms that rattle.

"Wait till your sweetness stings in aftertaste
And leaves the tongue unraveling sweets from sours.
You're after fruit—don't be so proud of flowers.
Wait for October in assured unhaste
Being grateful for these hours."

That was the way, old sir, you closed your letter
In the last season of straight-backboned life.
Clusters of apples hang—the bland, the bitter—
And mine are late. How can I praise you better
Here in the wind's knife?

Bermuda

Old man, come out in the sun,
The white blind of one o'clock!
Across the road a rusty cock
Stalks, his wars forgotten.

Here red and purple hang
From trees and tropic sky,
A cockscomb sunblaze, high—
Or the rains clang

On tin roof and gutterspout
And hot palms whistling.
Old man, stop rustling
Your shaking plumes, come out!

Rock Climbing

Higher than gulls' nests, higher than children go,
Scrambling and dangling to survey the sea,
   We crest the last outcropping strewn
      East of this island.

Now pell-mell, now stopping to pinch a finger
In an open fissure down which no sun glints,
   Where water gnaws and subsides, we comb
      As the tide rises

Each rock that locks us in a partial vision
Of the expanding, curved and eye-reflecting blue
   Which liberates but still hangs over
      Our minds' breathing.

As yet the gleams are steep and unexpected:
We study lichens like a dying scale,
   Silver as fishes; here crisp moss
      Moist in a crevice;

Then even lichens powder, and the rocks
Give way to sunny tables, dry escarpments,
   Each with its different texture, pocked
      Or smoothly sloping

Down to the pitch where barnacles or stain
Dark as a rust line show the heaving power
  Of water's shoulders, raised at night,
      Then wrested over.

And now the last rock! piled hugely up
And shoved to end a sprinkle like a jetty
  Of little boulders in the green-brown
      Irregular surface

Where seaweed shaped like coral swimming, kelp,
Pebbles and broken shells of clam or crab
  All shine or flicker up as down-watching
      We kneel and wonder.

Now balancing, laughing, brisk as children who
Spread out their arms and toe along a pole
  We skip from top to top, lift knees,
      Come out at angles

Until we have scaled it! stand aloft at last
With all the ocean for our freedom and
  Our meditation, all the swing
      Of limbs for glitter.

Warmed by the sun, tingling, with tired calves
And eyes of exultation we address
  The father of our knowledge, shrouded
      Faintly beyond us

At the lost line where wind is turned to water
And all is turned to light, dissolved or rinsed
   To silver where our eyes fish (gulls
         Sailing and falling

Out, out. . . .) And now the seabirds call
Far off, recalled by memories like hunger,
   Screech and return, flying the tides
         Of pure air inwards

To where their nests are, intimate and cold;
While standing on those cliffs we slowly rest
   And looking back to hillsides build
         Imaginary houses.

                 —DEER ISLE, MAINE

III

Blue

Spaces

For Thomas Hardy

(after reading "Nobody Comes," dated on my birthday)

But you were wrong that desolate dusk
    When up the street the crawl
    Of age and night grew tall
As a shadow-self leaning away
    From the gray religious husk
Of a streetlamp keeping watch above dead day.
    Another took some risk.

    You thought yourself alone
    In a world whose nearest ghost
    Was the alien pentecost
Of strumming telegraph, the throb
    Of a motor quickly gone—
While over the animal sea my outraged sob
    Took life from the same dawn.

Practicing for Death

1.

Monarch and fritillary, swallowtail—
Great butterflies red-brown or glossy black,
Spotted or striped or plain,
Each glistening with down—
I chased you through my earliest fields and back
Along a tangled track
To where the woods grew secret, dark and tall.

There you would disappear with a last hover,
Scurry or zigzag purposeless to the eye,
Witless and teasing, yet
Always beyond my net,
Beyond my fluttering hand that could not fly.
Brave alter-mystery,
Always you found some shadow for your cover.

Or I would watch you trembling on a branch
Open and close with pure control your wings
As if a steady hand
Slowly could wind, unwind
The coil that steeled those frail yet tensile springs,
As if unhurried breathings
Had drifted you aloft out of my reach.

Lost beyond reach—yet still I tried to follow
Down your close paths and into the sun again,
For what except to yield
All pleasures of the field
Into a single, gold and gathered grain?
To force the flash of vision
Under my grasp to fill that pulsing hollow?

And what if I garnered death, the fix of art,
Instead of the moving spark I chose to race?
When winter found my hoard
Pinned to a naked board,
Was it my own long-legged, sidelong grace
I had betrayed, the space
Of instant correspondence in the heart?

2.

For there were times, after long hours spent
In meadows smelling hot and dry of noon
Where every grass would stir
Shagged over with blue aster,
I would surprise you, dozing, fumbling drone.
Quickly my sliding prison
Would muffle you in clouds of blinding lint.

And I would pinch my net around that weed
You hung from, until beating up and out
In dense, bewildered strivings
You battered with your wings
And head against the deep net's lightstruck throat,

Or loosening your feet
Crawled up the folded shadows of its side.

Then carrying you as hopefully as an egg
Cradled in cotton, I would pause, advance
On cautious legs until
I begged someone to kill
The body I had pinioned in its dance—
Small, ignorant, intense
And homely engine of the whirligig.

Still in odd dreams I wonder, is it strength
Never to bear the final act of prey?
What native cowardice
Clamped me as in a vise
Before the oozing glamor of decay?
Veined, irradiant beauty,
I brought no stillness to your labyrinth.

Even the fields that beckoned then seemed wild,
Shimmering with sun-traps or cloud-plays.
Ribbons of violence
Wove round each naive sense—
How could I trust? When shall I learn to praise
Tracing you down dark ways
Again, live butterflies? ablaze, scared child!

Blue Spaces

1 | THE SUNDIAL

Take out of time that moment when you stood
On the far porch, a monolith of man,
And I raised one flag arm above my head:
Two statues crying out in stares of stone.

And take that moment when your flame-blue eyes
Blazed on me till true sunlight seemed to fail
And all our landscape fell away like lies:
The burr of bees, grass, flowers, the slow sundial.

And take that moment after kneeling speech—
"Rare things must be respected," your lips said—
When moveless I withheld myself from reach;
Unmoving, gave my need to fill your need.

Behind us in the garden the great sundial
Began to stretch its shadow toward afternoon.
Nothing was altered. Only we sat still,
Spent with sane joy beyond the bees' numb drone.

2 | THE GRAVEYARD

Where five old graves lay circled on a hill
And pines kept all but shattered sunlight out
We came to learn about
How each had sinned, loved, suffered, lost until
He met the other and grew somehow still.

Under those soughing, rumor-speaking trees
Full of dead secrets, on the August ground,
We leaned against a mound
Not touching; there, as we could, gave keys
To open midnight vaults that no one sees.

All that had shaped us thirty years or more
We tried to offer—not as brave youngsters do
Who need an echo, who
See in their fathers' sins a canceled score—
But as two grieving inmates tapping at the door.

Gifts of the self which were but bids for power,
Gifts of the innocent self—stripped, bound and torn—
A rare child wrongly born
And our best strivings turned, with age, half-sour:
Such darkness we unlocked within an hour.

Those five old graves lay speechless while the sun
Gradually stroked them with its flickering arm,
The smell of pines grew warm.
We walked away to watch a fresh stream run
As free as if all guilts were closed and done.

3 | THE RACETRACK

Under our stillness fled the same low hooves—
After, before, from the first morning when
We stood to watch the horses exercise.
Like a small sea the track dazzled our eyes:
Two riders shouting, flattening to run,
A spray of turf flung glistening toward the sun,
Stallions and fillies combing like distant waves.

Blind, pounding beasts came whirling through the mist,
Sweat on their flanks, their ankles wreathed in spume,
The day I told you of my loneliness;
Or I saw darkly out of such distress
As knocked my heart against its fragile room
Until our eyes touched and that light went home—
So we were one before we spoke or kissed.

Now that our bodies move and wake as one
That daybreak dream of horses has changed too
And we are free to say, as shadows scatter,
"Sound carries on this track as on deep water."
The trees shake out their leaves. We feel the slow
Rotation of a world in which we grow;
Slowly we learn our long wave's luminous motion.

Song: Staten Island Ferry

Stranger, in my arms last night
You lay and now the ferry
Is rocking at its slip.
I lean across the ship
(It bellows—we must hurry!)
Searching for you; you squint into the light.

Lost as the buildings ebb away,
The bridges loom and gather
And Liberty turns green,
Today you are only seen.
Last night the naked bather
Plunged through dark gleams and phosphorescent spray.

Humbly I touch your hand; you start
And smile on me in kindness—
Sea-captain on his child.
I fear some clipperish, wild
Blue mirrored in your blindness.
The ferry groans, returning to its heart.

In the Last Few Moments Came the Old German Cleaning Woman

Our last morning in that long room,
Our little world, I could not cry
But went about the senseless chores
—Coffee and eggs and newspapers—
As if your plane would never fly,
As if we were stopped there for all time.

Wanting to fix by ritual
The marriage we could never share
I creaked to stove and back again.
Leaves in the stiffening New York sun
Clattered like plates; the sky was bare—
I tripped and let your full cup fall.

Coffee scalded your wrist and that
Was the first natural grief we knew.
Others followed after years:
Dry fodder swallowed, then the tears
When mop in hand the old world through
The door pressed, dutiful, idiot.

A Little Vesper

Another day gone, and still
I haven't answered those letters
that clog my desk and heart.
The sky is a blown-up page
scribbled by swallows; the sun
drops in a pearl of mist
under an orange roof—
What am I hankering for?

Idly I hum this poem
as I wait for the tiny shriek
of a swallow outside, the whistle
of a leaf on my dry porch.
Sometimes it rains here. Letters
are piled up now like old snow
in the cramp of the spring evening—
Everyone sends his love.

And what do I want, ever,
more than these simple names
crying solicitude
in a black scrawl, beyond seas?
Swallows, it's time to fly home,
crawl in under the tiles
and bed with what we are—
breathe goodnight to the first strangers.

These High White Walls

So now to write the journal of this house,
these high white walls, this empty winter:
New scenes to disinter!
New ghosts to rouse!

Never a more stubborn dwelling-place
was bodied out with beds and chairs,
fleshed with familiars.
—Old empty face,

did you learn nothing from your dream of age?
Did no one laugh, make love or sing
to stamp your echoing
close with his image?

Let's call high festival, let's settle here,
break bread, kiss gently and converse—
Not one board answers.
Frozen panes stare.

In the House of the Dying

So once again, hearing the tired aunts
whisper together under the kitchen globe,
I turn away; I am not one of them.

At the sink I watch the water cover my hands
in a sheath of light. Upstairs she lies alone
dreaming of autumn nights when her children were born.

On the steps between us grows in a hush of waiting
the impossible silence between two generations.
The aunts buzz on like flies around a bulb.

I am dressed like them. Standing with my back turned
I wash the dishes in the same easy way.
Only at birth and death do I utterly fail.

For death is my old friend who waits on the stairs.
Whenever I pass I nod to him like the newsman
who is there every day; for them he is the priest.

While the birth of love is so terrible to me
I feel unworthy of the commonest marriage.
Upstairs she lies, washed through by the two miracles.

My Young Mother

My young mother, her face narrow
and dark with unresolved wishes
under a hatbrim of the twenties,
stood by my middleaged bed.

Still as a child pretending sleep
to a grownup watchful or calling,
I lay in a corner of my dream
staring at the mole above her lip.

Familiar mole! but that girlish look
as if I had nothing to give her—
Eyes blue—brim dark—
calling me from sleep after decades.

The Weather of Six Mornings

1.

Sunlight lies along my table
like abandoned pages.

I try to speak
of what is so hard for me

—this clutter of a life—
Puritanical signature!

In the prolonged heat, insects,
pine needles, birch leaves

make a ground bass of silence
that never quite dies.

2.

Treetops are shuddering
in uneasy clusters

like rocking water
whirlpooled before a storm.

Words knock at my breast,
heave and struggle to get out.

A black-capped bird
pecks on, unafraid.

Yield then, yield
to the invading rustle of the rain!

3.

All is closed in
by an air so rain-drenched

the distant barking of tied-up dogs
ripples to the heart of the woods.

Only a man's voice
refuses to be absorbed.

Hearing of your death
by a distant roadside

I wanted to erect some marker
though your ashes float out to sea.

4.

If the weather breaks
I can speak of your dying,

if the weather breaks,
if the crows stop calling

and flying low
(Again today there is thunder

outlying. . . .)
I can speak of your living,

the lightning-flash of meeting,
the green leaves waving at our windows.

5.

Yesterday a letter
spoke of our parting—

a kind of dissolution
so unlike this sudden stoppage.

Now all the years in between
flutter away like lost poems.

And the morning light is so delicate,
so utterly empty. . . .

at high altitude, after long illness,
breathing in mote by mote a vanished world. . . .

Rest.
A violin bow, a breeze

just touches the birches.
Cheep—a new flute

tunes up in a birch top.
A chipmunk's warning skirrs. . . .

Whose foot disturbs these twigs?
To the sea of received silence

why should I sign
my name?